With best wishes
to ---

Ron Curley

ImpPress

Lockdown Scribblings

By

Ron Impey
Nick Day
David Pearl
Alex Pearl
Ken Mullen
Graham Smith
Ian Maxted
Andrew Impey

Published by the authors and ImpPress

© Ron Impey, Nicholas Day, David Pearl, Alex Pearl, Graham Smith, Ian Maxted, Ken Mullen and Andrew Impey, 2021

LockdownScribblings@virginmedia.com

Typesetting and formatting by **Abdul Rehman**

For all our loved ones.

Foreword

Quite a number of people must have thought of composing poetry during Lockdown. The offerings in this collection would, however, never have been written had a copywriter, Ken Mullen, not sent 'Ovid for Covid' to my brother, Alex. He forwarded it to me and I, in turn, to Ron Impey, a Classicist. And that unlocked the versifying Muse. Ron responded with a learned rejoinder and, before the week was up, he was producing poems. I also tried my hand and we were away. A request for other contributions produced some more, while the indefatigable Ron made up for a lifetime of non-poetic writing by going into industrial production, a sort of Nightingale Ode Project, if Mr Keats will excuse the phrase.

None of this is to minimise or ignore the tragic side of Covid. We paused a few times to wonder about the propriety of penning humorous verse at such a time. But a cursory survey of the Press and media shows how many 'lifestyle' and similar articles have been written about these difficult months. To write light verse is not to ignore the many sufferings that tens of thousands have endured. This has been a dark time; yet, there is a need to laugh and find a release. These scribblings are one way of finding a way of relieving the gloom of a pandemic.

The events of these months have also provided much material for satire or, at a lesser level, a bit of a giggle. This probably culminated in the Cummings Saga, the most infamous road trip in political history, concerning which everything that could be said has been. Where some of these verses touch on it, we hope to have struck something of a novel note, or at least a rhyming one.

So, we trust that these pieces and the few parodies we have added will raise a smile. Nobody knows the extent to which Covid has changed our lives for good, but whatever the outcome, this slim volume documents how a few people in 2020 reacted when they put fingers to keyboard and went into rhyming mode and mood.

David Pearl

Table of Contents

All poems by Ron Impey unless another author is shown.

All illustrations are by Nick Day.

Introduction

The Muse which inspired the writing of the items in the present miscellany seems almost to have deserted me when composing an Introduction. David's eloquent Foreword explains the motivation and rationale of this project: the individual items must speak for themselves.

The subject-matter relates, of course, as the title suggests, to this unusual, unforgettable, and maybe unique period of pandemic through which we are living. Contemporary readers will appreciate the obvious and sometimes less obvious allusions – which may prove a little more cryptic to any possible future readers. Inevitably, political figures and the government receive a few wry digs – which seems to go with the job and does not reflect any political bias. It all helps the perplexed citizen to let off steam.

There are other, subtler allusions to literature, music and who knows what else? The writer may not always be aware of how his personal experiences affect his writing; the reader is invited to exercise his/her Imagination!

There are some blank pages at the end for the reader to become the writer and to personalise this booklet by scribbling a personal contribution in verse, prose, or illustration – or entering up family news – and then, maybe, passing it on.

I am indebted to the others who have contributed to this effort, particularly to David for his unfailing good counsel and congeniality in our zoom comradeship, to Alex for his unstinted and helpful suggestions, to Nick for his superb illustrations and advice, and to my wife Judy for valuable practical assistance and patient encouragement. It brings me great pleasure, too, that my great-nephew Andrew Impey (author of "The Epic Adventure: A Journey Across North America") accepted my invitation to contribute a poem.

We have derived great pleasure from composing these 'scribblings' - which we hope you, too, will enjoy.

PS The capricious Muse dictates one extra, final, and perhaps rather corny verse:

In times of stress, when strength seems almost gone,
Just smile, keep calm, - and carry on.

Ron Impey

WHEN...?

When shall we all meet again

In springtime, summer, sun, or rain?

When will it end, this horrid trouble,

Lockdown, quarantine, social bubble?

When shall we move about with ease

And mingle with anyone we please?

When will Boris (and Dom?) say "yes",

When will we all be free from mess?

ONE

One can flout the rules without a care

And advise one's boss not to give the sack

To one who might possibly pay him back.

If not forced by law to apologise

Why shouldn't one simply just despise

Those humbler folk who respect the rules

And those who for honour's sake resign – the fools?!

R.I.P.

Do not make me a statue when I decease.

Remember me. May I rest in peace.

When statues topple and rage decreases,

The plinth remains; the rest is in pieces.

FALLEN IDOLS

Beautiful icon or shoddy plastic

Is all the same to the iconoclastic.

HUE CARES

The colour of skin doesn't matter to me:

I am what I am – just nice and carefree.

The statue of Edward Colston erected in 1895 was pulled down in Bristol in June 2020 by anti-racism protesters for his part in the slave trade. This was followed by questions about the suitability of other statues in Britain.

HOME THOUGHTS FROM AWAY

(With apologies to Robert Browning)

Oh, to be in England with April
lockdown there

And whoever wakes in
England sees, some morning,
unaware,

By the fox's poo 'neath the
garden hedge

The first green shoots of our
tiny veg,

While the pigeons mate on
our beech tree bough

In lockdown — now!

And after April, May must
follow

With food for hungry mouths
to swallow,

Now things for home delivery
are sorted.

No planes, no cars, no noise,
we are in clover

Unworldly calm, so still, I am
transported ...

That's my dear spouse who
yells commands twice over

Lest, dozing deep in blissful
silent rapture,

The first request I sadly failed
to capture!

And, though my hair grows
longer by the day,

Who's there to see while we
can hide away?

And Zoom or Skyping we
could always shirk,

Far sweeter than this masked
commute to work!

FREE TO RELAX

Is it better to be locked down here at home out of reach

Or to relax with millions down there on the beach?

WEIGHT FOR THE GONDOLA

Over-weight passengers could make gondolas sink.

Before you board, please carefully think.

THE POLITICAL LADDER									
It's not fair to call	B	O	R	I	S	L	A	Z	Y
Nor maybe to mutter	D	O	M	S	C	R	A	Z	Y
To tinker with a word	D	E	M	S	C	R	A	Z	Y
Can seem rather absurd	D	E	M	O	C	R	A	Z	Y
And a good concept	D	E	M	O	C	R	A	C	Y
Can be rendered quite crazy	D	O	M	O	C	R	A	C	Y
Or	D	O	R	O	C	R	A	C	Y
Simply hazy.	B	O	R	O	C	R	A	C	Y

O DEAR ME

O dear me
How will it be
Without Dom-dom
Here advising me?

O dear me
One-two-three
Must I sit on another knee
Or stand on my feet
And just be me?

O dear me
Four-five-six
MPs will be up to all their tricks!
How will I be carried through
My next big fix?

O dear me
Seven-eight-nine
The coming new decisions

Will be all mine.

(M)ASK THE EXPERTS

A professor of Prosopokalypsology from his reasearches reveals

Face-coverings can cause problems with meals.

Unyielding mask-wearers, though well-meaning folk,

Without easy food-inlets can splutter and choke.

His colleague in Prosopokalypsychology – a rarefied field –

Claims studies of remote jungle tribes can yield

Proof that the prolonged wearing of masks

Inhibits mental dexterity in manifold tasks,

A PhD student has gone the whole hog

With total face blackout, his life in a fog

Of utter involvement in locked-in zeal

Using tubes to drink and eat each meal.

His muffled pronouncements are not very clear

But DV his results might come out next year.

Deirdre Lovelook, an expert in the aesthetic history of masks,

From visiting art galleries and from similar tasks,

Says of all the statues she has ever re-viewed

More than veiled females she prefers the male nude.

A nameless bank-robber thinks that obscuring his face

Might well help to make him harder to trace.

Experts, it seems, may not see eye-to-eye

But to form an opinion we all must try.

Though Gove and Johnson don't quite coincide,

The official UK rule has taken the side

Of those experts who, with clever insight,

Declare face-covers can catch virus droplets – or might

Ministerial Menu

For Starters:

1. Potage Boris – the cumin-enriched cloudy soup of the day, accompanied by our popular "Priti" paté.

Main course:

1. Rishi kebab – chef's choice – a tasty s'nack (in the event of a problem you can claim money back).

2. Hand-reared cock -au-cabinet govignon - a healthy choice now (and when covid has gone)

3. Locally-sourced domestic raabit stew which rivals cuisine from the foreign EU.

Dessert (maybe to follow the above):

1. A specially tempting thornberry tart

2. Apple-corbyn pie (a speciality art)

3. The intoxicating new trifle nandy

Finally

1. A glass of Keirsh(!) a most subtle brandy.

NONSENSE ON STILT

They came from many miles away,

A deal to sign, some bills to pay,

But unbeknown to Eastern hosts,

The Truss team had a card to play.

In Tokyo it was thought a breeze,

Some tariffs here, and there some fees,

But unbeknown to Eastern hosts,

The Truss team had a brief for cheese.

Others said, this deal we'll build on,

To strengthen ties with loyal Nippon,

But unbeknown to Eastern hosts,

The Truss team only thought of Stilton.

"It has emerged that Liz Truss, the international trade secretary, backed away from signing a historic post-Brexit trade deal with Japan last week in support of a British cheese worth 0.007% of total UK exports to the country."

[The Times 12 August 2020]

WHY TRAVEL TO THE PEAKS?

The Lammergeier is the Bearded Vulture, one of Europe's largest raptors and an extremely rare visitor to Britain. It appeared in the Peak District in July this year.

The eagle was in ancient times thought of as the special bird of omen of Jove (Jupiter). The linnet is a small bird of the finch family.

*Flecker wrote a poem about **"A Linnet who had lost her way".***

A Lammergeier sighting in the Peaks has occurred

-a rare British visit from this majestic bird.

What could this bearded vulture signify?

Might it be a well-masked spy

From some foreign power with evil intent

To cause us a cyber predicament?

From Russia, from China? We wonder "Why?"

Pique at UK's break with Huawei?

Perhaps from some lofty peak it scans

And peeks at our secret sites and plans.

Could it be that this bird of Jove

Was meant to warn a Johnson or Gove?

From the heights of Olympus was it sent

With some special advice for parliament?

Is this vulture an omen for us today

Or, like that linnet, did it just lose its way?

Was its vision – or mind- not at its best?

Was it flying, off course, for an eyesight test?

LOCKDOWN EASING

Part - 01

Come into the garden, Claude;

I've been waiting here for thee.

Come into the garden, Claude,

For a cup of "you and me"!

BUT DO NOT come too close to me, Claude,

Don't sneeze or cough or spray

Beyond that white two-metre board.

I'll look the other way.

There's a seat marked out for you, my love,

By that yonder apple-tree,

Where, with Bramleys hanging up above,

We have chatted merrily.

Just give the wink to me - please do! -

If you want a little cake.

I'll toss one gaily straight to you!

They're your favourite ones I make.

(In fact, I baked a lot last night,

Practised tossing skilfully,

In case it should vanish out of sight

Or drop right in your tea.)

What fun it is – just you and I

Post-lockdownishly meeting up like this.

It's really worth this gallant try.

And now perhaps a hug and kiss?

Part - 02

Come, come again to my garden, Claude

For some further "you and me".

I never feel lonely or ever bored

With you nearby sipping tea.

Yes! You can come somewhat closer now!

One metre apart! Did you see?

How I yearn to stroke your handsome brow

And sit upon your noble knee!

Soon, let us pray, I can hold you tight

'neath the shelter of my bramley tree

Quaffing Earl Grey far into the night

Ever nearer, my Claude, to thee!

WATCH WEIGHT

I don't know much about vitamins and that

But they say that, if I eat too much fat,

There's a danger I might just become obese

Though, if I take care, my size should decrease.

Is Boris thinking of passing a law

To stop us consuming more and more

Of foods which look so tempting to eat

But ought to be just a "no" or rare treat?

A PORTLY CHANCE

Obesity is what they call it when BMI's too high,

Though statuesque is more polite when noting girth of thigh.

Well padded is another version that some choose to employ,

Or well proportioned might avoid offence to your big boy.

Love handles an affectionate way of sizing up your beau,

When overweight is too direct an epithet to throw.

Stout fellow often does the trick when other words elude,

Or rather plump while admiring an old Velasquez nude.

So, now we have the virus and its ravages to beat,

We recognise the deleterious costs of fat and meat.

If you're to improve health outcomes and not become a stat,

Shun these euphemisms and stay thin and not too fat.

FACT & FICTION: LIES & TRUTH

TRUTH - ECONOMY, TINKERING, TWISTING, DECAY

RELATIVE TRUTH, POST-TRUTH...

Mr Trump, it is claimed, has told 20,000 lies.

But, never mind – "It's all fake news!" he replies.

Trumped-up news is nothing new

Which I can't a*bide* - *n*or can you?

Future news no-one can tell –

As both Joe and Donald know full well.

"OK, I've twitted in a different way:

What was true last week isn't true today.

It's you mis-hear, not me mis-speak:

I'm never wrong - you're a freak."

(to the tune of Nellie the Elephant)

Donald the President packed his trunk

And said goodbye to the "Circus".

Off he went with a trumpety trump,

Trump, Trump, Trump.............

KEEP GOING

"Don't think of falling, think of skating, Dad!"

Wise words, in truth, from a young child of six!

"Let's get on the floor once again, my lad,

And start to rebuild our tumbled-down bricks!"

The boy in the painting by John Millais

Watches his bubbles as they float then burst,

Absorbed and absorbing, the same every day.

Bubbles go: fun and sparkles come first.

West Ham, your dreams may fade and die,

Despite ace players like Antonio;

One day your fame may reach the sky,

As your bubbles for ever you blow!

Centenarian Tom raised millions of pounds

Zimmering along on his garden forays,

Then dubbed by the Queen in Windsor's grounds

Sir Thomas Moore. One of his very good days!

Aphrodite, they say, was born

From the foam of the bubbling sea.

The bonds of Love cannot be torn

Tho' we be "bubbled" separately.

Muddle, fuddle, toil, and trouble.

When shall we be free to hug again?

Blow away our constraining bubble.

Sunshine will follow the rain!

HAIRCUTS

My barber donned a visor
round his head.

His breathing was thus not
widely spread

But deflected down on my
face instead.

Now, like his customer, he
wears a mask,

Both of them sharing the
breathing task.

My wife asked me to trim her
hair the other day.

She seemed not very keen to
– but why she didn't say.

I tried to keep her sprits up
by chatting cheerily,

Offered paracetamol and a
good strong cup of tea.

I trimmed the hair upon her
neck nice and straight and
clean;

The front I levelled up and
made it shapelier than it had
been.

She survived with relief and a
surprised look upon her face

And expressed her grateful
thanks (but of a tip there was
no trace).

Next day: "You've had your
hair done! How lovely!" said a
friend.

"My husband did it for me,"
said my wife. I've really set a
trend!

Don't go to Brutus the barber,
you fool!

His is the most unkindest cut
of all.

BEN THE BOXER

Ambition, Experience, & Fulfilment

Ben has been learning to box from a book he bought.

He's progressing well – completely self-taught.

Yesterday he knocked himself out – for the count of ten.

I think I'll buy a different book for Ben.

Undeterred by such a trifling thing

When rules allowed he entered the ring.

In his first triumphant longed-for bout

Alas he tripped and was again knocked out.

Since then he's donned the wedding ring

And joined a choir and tries to sing.

But, still anxious to use his manual skills,

He makes decorative boxes for window-sills.

KEEPING PATHWAYS OPEN

I walk along the river paths each day
And have made a sort of game to play.
I say "hello" to each passerby
And make a note if they reply.
Those who do are certainly more
But there are some who just ignore –
Perhaps they have their headphones on
Or else their good manners have gone.

Some days I count instead
Cyclists with a helmet on head.
The majority are suitably protected
Tho' my observation has detected
Many, alas, of the other kind
Who left their helmets or wits behind.

There are plenty of joggers too,
Some vigorous types, and others who
Stagger along quite out of puff
Ready to admit they've had enough.
I greet them with a friendly "Hi"
And the nicest and ablest mostly reply.

Dogs abound with their human friends.

I am not quite sure of recent trends

Or canine breeds of the present day.

Cocker Spaniels and Labradors are in vogue they say

With the Yorkshire Terrier and the Cockapoo

And the Golden Retriever and the Dachshund, too.

It's useful to exercise my brain

As I wander along in sun or rain

Alive to every event around

While alert to any stuff on the ground

Like tree-roots, cow pats, and refuse too

(It's sad what some other people do).

NON-HOLIDAY PLANS

Peut-être éviterons-nous Paris en été
Nor cruise on the Loire or the Thames for a day.

Firenze, Bologna, Milano, o Roma?
Non andiamo there – and never to Cromer!

Wir fahren nicht nach Heidelberg this year.
Let's cancel the Lake District too, my dear.

Δεν θα πάμε φέτος στην Ελλάδα
(pron. dthen tha parmeh fetos steen elladtha)
Or not go to Bournemouth or Hove, if you'd rather.

Ad alias terras non faciemus iter
Nor visit the gym to make ourselves fitter.

We zullen niet reizen naar Amsterdam
Nor pay respects to my birthplace West Ham.

¡ Qué lástima no ir a sunny Spain!
¡ Qué pena! Let's just stay at home in the rain.
Yes! Let's stay in das Loch Doon und write silly verse
In franglais etcetera! It could be worse.

Holiday plans are all topsy-turvy this year.
Non-holiday plans can be made without fear.

Could non-holiday plans go topsy-turvy too?
I don't know where we'd go then! Do you?

Perhaps we'll avoid Paris in summer
Nor cruise on the Loire or the Thames for a day.
Florence, Bologna, Milan, or Rome?
We won't go there – and never to Cromer!

We will not travel to Heidelberg this year.
Let's cancel the Lake District too, my dear.
We will not go this year to Greece
Or not go to Bournemouth or Hove, if you'd rather.

We will not travel to other lands
Nor visit the gym to make ourselves fitter.
We will not visit Amsterdam
Nor pay respects to my birthplace West Ham.

A pity not to go to sunny Spain!
Alas! Let's just stay at home in the rain.
Yes! Let's stay in Loch Doon and write silly verse
In "franglais" and so on! and it could be worse.

RETURN TO CHURCH MEETING

Do not when meeting give a
rapturous greeting.

Do not kiss or embrace or
hug: just give a smile, sweet
not smug.

"Share a stare" is a safe way
of exchanging our blessings
today.

Do not sit close to others too
tight; leave a gap to the left
and to the right.

Before passing others please
glance to avoid spoiling a
spiritual trance.

Consult the official expert to
ask whether or not you should
wear a mask.

Despite your melodious voice,
do not sing: demonstrate joy
with a muted zing.

If you have a hum book, quietly
hum – though musicians out
front may e.g. strum.

If you cannot stay dumb
but must speak, official
permission please seek.

Remember: "Chansons sans
paroles" are potentially good
for the soul.

Preachers will not explosively
preach sending forth words of
far-flung reach.

No fire and brimstone today:
we must eschew dangerous
spray.

Those at home shut in their
room should be ready to meet
by zoom.

PS Frequently wash or gel –
or else you risk going not to
heaven!

FAMILY ACTIVITY

In the lounge there's Jess doing ballet

While Sophie head-stands on the floor,

Baby Beth looks on surprised at the mêlée

Having crawled at speed through the door.

Lucy, serene, multi-tasking,

Takes everything well in her stride.

Iain in "Siberian bunker" now working

Will be soon cooking dinner inside.

Cedric and Jo have skyped in now

With exuberant Georges full of fun

While busily playing Ben wonders how

His big brother can so rapidly run.

Performance

Lucy and Jo play a piano duet

To start our best performance yet.

On the fiddles are Jo, Luce, and Grandpa;

Iain, Cedric, and Jess on guitar.

Jess and Sophie perform dance and ballet,

Gran is in charge of the family play.

IT'S ALL GREEK TO ME

Dud: This corona thing is a right pain

Pete: You're not wrong there. I was only thinking the other day what a right pain in the derrière – if you'll excuse my French – what a right pain in the derrière this wretched thing has become.

Dud: What gets me is they don't even tell us why they call it coronavirus.

Pete: I can tell you why. It's because they are completely in the dark about it. So they've had to call it something wondrous and ethereal to mask their total ignorance.

Dud: Wondrous and ethereal?

Pete: Yes, wondrous and ethereal. Of course they had to have a bit of a brain-storm to come up with the name. And then as if by some divine providence, some bright spark would have come up with the idea of calling it… "coronavirus".

Dud: On account of it being wondrous and ethereal?

Pete: On account of it being wondrous and ethereal.

Dud: So where does the name actually come from, Pete?

Pete: Well, there you've got me. But, if I were a gambling man, which of course I'm not…I would put my money on the name itself being of Latin derivation.

Dud: Latin derivation?

Pete: Yes, Latin derivation….You see, there's nothing quite as wondrous and ethereal as a bit of Latin derivation….I mean to say, this Prime Minister loves his Latin.

Dud: I thought he loved the ladies.

Pete: Aside from loving the ladies, he also has a bit of a thing about Latin.

Dud: You mean a little bit of Latin on the side?

Pete: Yes – a bit of Latin on the side....He loves his Latin. Can't get enough of the Latin. Only the other day he came up with a lovely little gem. He can't help himself. He's always getting the urge.

Dud: He's known for his urges, isn't he?

Pete: Yes, Dud, he's known for his urges. He has his fair share of urges.

Dud: So what was this lovely little gem?

Pete: The lovely little gem in question was "veni, vidi, vici."

Dud: Not being conversant with Latin, would you mind transliterating?

Pete: I will even go so far as elucidating. Roughly translated veni vidi vici means I came, I saw, and did all kinds of unmentionables.

Dud: I see.

Pete: Of course, he's not the only one to be partial to this Latin. The queen likes her Latin, too.

Dud: Does she?

Pete: She's very partial to a bit of Latin is Her Highness. When she had that fire at Windsor Castle. You remember that, don't you?.

Dud: Oh yes. Dreadful business.

Pete: Indeed....Well, she didn't describe that year as being particularly nasty.

Dud: Didn't she?

Pete: No. She called it "annus horribilis".

Dud: Annus horribilis? Would you mind soliciting again?

Pete: Certainly....It's Latin. In other words, an extremely wondrous and ethereal way of saying that her year was a bit of a bummer.

Dud: Bit of a bummer?

Pete: Yes. You see, the thing about Latin is that, whatever you say, it will always sound wondrous and ethereal.

Dud: Seems a bit funny to me wanting to speak a language nobody understands.

Pete: Well, if you can speak in a way that very few people can actually understand, you are very well qualified to be Prime Minister.

Dud: Why's that, then?

Pete: Well, just think about it. If you were Prime Minister, which, thank goodness, you aren't, and you were asked a very difficult question which you didn't know the answer to, what would you say?

Dud: I suppose I'd be stumped for words.

Pete: Well, you wouldn't be stumped for words when you can answer in Latin. Because, by answering in Latin, you'll be giving an answer that no one will understand.

Dud: And I suppose you'd be confusing everyone in an ethereal and wondrous way.

Pete: You would indeed be confusing everyone in an ethereal and wondrous way. And that, in a rather round-about way in answer to your original question, is why the wretched virus is named coronavirus.

Dud: It's all Greek to me, Pete.

Pete: Well actually, Dud, you're quite right. It is, I believe, also Greek in derivation. Of course, the Greeks were a very clever bunch. Very clever indeed.

Dud: Interesting that you say that. Because there's a very ancient Greek gentleman who used to have a kebab shop near me until he was closed down by Health and Safety. That wasn't so clever, was it, Pete?

Pete: Well, you have to remember that some extremely ancient Greeks do unfortunately suffer from dementia.

Dud: Dementia?

Pete: Yes. Dementia. The funny thing about dementia – and there's not a lot that's funny about dementia – but the funny thing is that dementia is actually Latin, you know. (FADE)

JEEVES AND THE VIRUS

Bertie: "Jeeves, I need your advice. About the virus whatnot."

Jeeves: *"Covid 19, sir."*

"No, I'm not asking you about port vintages, it's this health scare. You see, the chaps at the Drones are worried we might have to close the place for the duration. Fearful rumpus after dinner, everyone shouting and saying the Plague would get us and we couldn't risk giving it to each other. Blind panic. Well, except for Biffy who said he'd forgotten to read the 'papers for a month. So a smidgeon of your sage advice would not go amiss."

"I profess no expertise, sir, but I would point out that the young appear not to be vulnerable. And the average age of your Club members is not much higher than the Poet's 'three and twentieth year', Perhaps this could be drawn to their attention."

"Well, that is comforting, Jeeves. But what about the risk of spreading it to the older club servants?"

"As I understand the scientific papers, it is unclear whether that form of transmission is happening. But the safest thing is if they keep a distance from members."

"But they always do that, Jeeves. None of them wants to risk a bread roll at close quarters, Bingo's aim is dreadful and the staff never seem keen on approaching too close."

"There we are, sir. And finally, remove the newspapers. Mr Biffen has adopted a sound course. I find most of the comment and so-called news to be most misleading and liable to induce panic and neurosis."

"Consider it done, Jeeves! Perhaps a medicinal g & t to ward off the bugs would be in order?"

JEEVES AND JENRICK

Bertie: "Jeeves, your counsel is again required. It's this Jenrick cove I'm reading about."

Jeeves: "Indeed, sir. A gift to my profession. I applaud his acquisition of properties since they all require some expert upkeep."

"Well, never mind that. It's the dinner story that gets me. People don't seem to understand how to behave."

"It is true he has been greatly criticised."

"No, no Jeeves, it's table manners I'm talking about."

"Sir?"

"Absolutely! Here he is, told to go and chomp his way through some half heated concoction in order to keep the troops happy and he finds himself seated next to this ghastly oik."

"Not a little tough, sir?"

"Perhaps the chicken was, but my point is we've all been there. Happens at the Drones occasionally. Some friend of Catsmeat can't find a seat and comes and sits down next to Bertram and jaws about dandelions or unguents for the next hour. Same as this Desmond chap. Comes and whips out his phone and insists on showing his holiday slides, or whatever."

"And you think the minister was being polite?"

"Exactly. A well brought up young chap, he looks at it attentively and wishes he was somewhere else. Then the bore tries to get him to visit, rather like my Aunts do, and this Jenrick says yes, he will, but is desperate to find some excuse to get out of it. 'Ah', he says' 'you've made some sort of application, sorry old chap, I'm In purduli, cheerio, must fly.' Now what's wrong with that?"

"I confess, you put it most eloquently, sir. Manners Maketh Man."

"Precisely my point and I'm glad you agree, Jeeves. Just keep a look out for the Desmond blighter and warn me if you ever see him lurking round the corner. You can't be too safe."

JEEVES AND EXAMS

Bertie: "Jeeves, I have not yet asked you about the exam imbroglio."

Jeeves: *"A most apt word to choose, if I may say so, sir."*

"You may, indeed, Italian, I imagine, for almighty lash-up."

"A passable definition, certainly."

"But, what I don't understand is why these grades matter. In my day, it wasn't the done thing to assess attainment, even less boast about it. You didn't have to pass exams, even at Oxford. A Gentleman's Degree was quite acceptable. O tempora, O mores, I suppose."

"I am sure the great Cicero may well have viewed it thus, sir."

"And if they are all concerned with these grades, why can't they just accept the beaks' assessments? After all, if they all get prizes, where is the harm?"

"It is a viewpoint that seems to have prevailed today."

"Now, prizes, Jeeves, that's another matter. Did I ever tell you that when I was a junior Bertram I won the Scripture-Knowledge prize at my kids' school?"

"You have sometimes alluded to the achievement."

"Well, that was an award worth having and it has caused much jealousy, I can tell you. Gussie maintains to this day that I secured it through unlawful means, a vile slander. I knew those Kings of Judah sideways and backwards. Never worked as hard at the old revision thing as before that test."

"I think that is the point the students make today, They feel they were robbed of their due."

"Well, then I'm with them, Jeeves. If this Williamson deprived them of their rightful portion, their due inheritance and the entry to the promised land, then they should get it nem con and no delay. Now you have put it on the same level as the Scripture-Knowledge prize, all is clear. A celebratory glass of bubbly is definitely in order!"

THE SONG OF HIGHER WAFFLE

If you ask me 'how speaks Johnson,?'

At the time of Covid crisis,

Who is upright at the lectern

When the daily news is given?

How are graphs and grim statistics

Broadcast to the daily masses?

Do they use the old smoke signals?

Or another means of talking

Power to truth and obfuscation,

Maybe through some thought transference

Or subliminal persuasion.

Then at five you must watch TV

From the comfort of your tepee,

How the Chiefs or else their minions

Inform Brits of facts and figures

Talking of their huge departments,

Triumphs huge but no disasters.

Flanked by experts all sagacious

(Save for those who contradict us.)

Then you'll see the patient journos

Waiting to add their tuppence worth

With a question plus another

If they haven't annoyed Hancock,

Or Grant Schapps or some such person

Holding office in Cabinet.

Questions asked but seldom answered

As our Chiefs swerve, twist and bluster

Hoping that the masses don't spot

How the query stays unresolved.

This is how the news is given,

This is how the line's transmitted,

This is how health propaganda

Goes out daily to the People.

This is what our elders broadcast,

This is now our Higher Waffle.

LETTERS TO AN M.P.

If doctors take the Hippocratic oath

Can politicians sign a hypocritic oath?!

My dad taught me we should trust them both.

Reply

I find your "humour" rather absurd.

Just trust us all till we break our word.

If it's legal now to break the law to a specific, limited degree,

May I throttle just one particular individual who's been annoying me?

Reply

You should always, of course, seek to obey the law

-Unless we amend it – that's for sure.

Avoid hasty action, whatever you do.

See your annoying friend first and talk it through.

A NATIONAL ROLL CALL

Throughout these isles they came to queue

To buy up paper for the loo,

A curious necessity

To purchase in such quantity.

You'd think they might already own

Sufficient rolls to use or loan,

For surely they were not so stingy

They used to replace each one singly?

But queue they did throughout the lands

To have the joy of laying hands,

And hope they wouldn't break their necks

While fighting for even more Andrex.

So, having lost their self-control

To build their towers of spare bog roll,

They need no more to buy a crate,

For theirs is but to sit and wait,

And for the sake of our great Nation

Avoid the curse of constipation.

KEEPING UP WITH THE RULES

If you don't lock-down when you ought
Can you be locked-up if you're caught?

If your face is not properly masked,
How do you answer when asked?
"My mask is at home. I left it behind."?
Or act all vacant or out of your mind?
It's best to consult with my friend Joe
Who was fined on the spot. He should know!

How many friends at a time can you meet
Four, six, eight, or half the street?
No doubt the details have been clearly said
But all the changes don't stay in my head.
It was a bit reassuring the other day
That the cabinet chap himself couldn't say
When asked to explain on the BBC
For mystified listeners like you and me.

Ada says we must all ride a bike.
She got this news from her friend Mike.
You first just contact your own GP
Then collect your machine from the pharmacy.
It's fifty years since I've ridden a bike
But Ada says "It's not what you like!
You'll get a refresher down at the gym.
You'll love it, gran! Don't look grim!
You'll be cruising along without a care
With designer helmet looking quite debonair!"

Zooming along on her bike
Past those who jog or hike
Gran is an aboundingly graceful sight,
A two-wheeled transport of delight.

Our friend Amanda's new shoes are pink
To match her designer mask, we think.

We'll soon need a visa to enter Kent
By decree, Ada says, of *Gover*nment.
Something to do with a no-Brexit deal
Or thousands of lorries heading for Deal?
(Not sure if that's bogus or really real.)

" But don't the EU want us any more?
Did Ursula, after their last supper, show Boris the door?
Was it something he did, or didn't do?
What will it mean for me and you?"

NON-EXAMS 2020

I was no good at Mafs wiv ol' Miss Bird.

"Wake up!" she'd say. "You're in a daze!"

Then my mates went round and 'ad a word.

Would you Adam and Eve it – we all got A's!

Dear Parent,

In entering up each predicted grade

An inadvertent, human mistake was made.

Our students were not entered for French, as we said,

But all have good grades for Finnish instead.

We advise they accept this odd situation,

Grateful for such a rare qualification.

In view of national lockdown & school closures the Government cancelled GCSE & GCE.A.Level exams. Grades were based on predictions by schools. There were various complications.

LOCK DOWN/KNOCK BACK

The rolling English drunkard, he might wait till Kingdom come

But the pubs remain in lockdown

For beer, whisky, wine, and rum.

Or for porter, or for water, you can hammer on the door,

But the Landlord's home with boxsets,

For the English pub's no more.

Not for sipping, not for quizzing, not for hanging out for hours,

The dart board's shut, the TV blank,

They've binned the plastic flowers.,

And, worst of all for CAMRA types and connoisseurs of ale,

The barrels all got emptied out

The bitter, stout, and pale.

They flowed into Old Albion's drains, a dreadful waste of beer,

As if the Puritans had come

To do away with cheer.

But Hark! The sounds of popping corks accompany a shout,

For Boris has spoke at last,

"On Four July, come out, come out!"

Enjoy your independence, a true red-letter day,

For topers, boozers, tipplers too,

To pub crawl and make hay.

"Drink, my hearties, drink your fill, and then a little more!

Joy unconfined, just open wide

And down your throats we'll pour!

GETTING BACK TO SCHOOL & WORK

I don't want to go back to school.

It's better at home. Now I've got pink hair

Miss will say "Oh! That's against the rule!"

And all the class will laugh and stare.

I don't need Maths or History and all that stuff.

We done too much grammar wiv old Shaky Bill;

Science, geography, sport? I've had enough!

I wish, how I wish I could be at home still.

My dad's still "working from home", they say.

"Shirking" more like for most of the day.

He's cross with me now my hair's gone pink.

Next week I'll dye it green, I think.

CELEBRATE WITH RESTRAINT

My friend Deirdre's gone
drinking again!

I'm rather concerned it may
addle her brain.

Even after drinking a single
gin

Her face gets suffused with a
vacuous grin,

But, after she's swigged two,
three, or four,

There's no holding Deirdre
back any more.

With four gins and a whisky
she gets quite frisky

And with any more booze
Deirdre's not good news –

Leaping on tables, all out of
control,

Adopting a most unladylike
role (roll?),

Grabbing the guys and
making them dance,

Not giving her Simon even a
glance.

These days she makes all her
flat-mates cringe,

Including me, though I am
studying "binge"

As a special topic for my
psycho' degree

-With special reference. now,
to Deirdre.

Is it her subconscious id, alter
ego...?

Freud, Jung, or our Prof.
would probably know.

Or is she sublimating an
unconscious desire

As she whirls and leaps higher
and higher

To give up all those thoughts
of degrees

And to aspire to a life on the
flying trapeze?

Whatever it is, I really don't
think

I'll join dear Deirdre in one
more drink.

UNIVERSITY LIFE

I went to University

To get a good degree,

Then found that in adversity

I was cooped up with thee.

Within a flat not very big,

With kitchenette so sparse,

And no room for a shindig,

To meet my online class.

They made us stay for Christmas,

But it didn't really matter,

We didn't need to make a fuss,

We'd stay all day and natter.

And then there came the second term

When you and I got married.

Relationship now good and firm

We're glad we stayed and tarried.

With a wee bairn on the way

We've yet to meet a tutor

In the flesh, but still we hope and pray

That we still have a future.

Perhaps one day they'll let us out

To end incarceration.

And as we leave we'll surely shout,

On walking to the station,

"You wanted us to grow up fast

When sending us to college,

And that's a test we surely passed,

For, to our certain knowledge,

We came as two and left as three

To sail on Life's Great Voyage,"

THE ZOOMY BLUES

I get up in the mornin'
And wonder what's the day today.
Sittin' over coffee,
Countin' up the furlough pay,

When I get an email
"Wanna Zoom?"
Well, what d'you say?
And I slip on a decent shirt,
Hell, I haven't shaved
But that ain't cause no hurt.

Got the Zoomy Blues,
Like I never had before.
When I see old staff from Allied,
Every single one a bore.
Or the gals from kindergarten,
Now they're grannies out in Pinner,
Who say they can't remember me,
And was I ever thinner?

Gotta end this lockdown,
And defy the Docs and doomsters,
Who would have us sittin' here for life
At mercy of the Zoomsters.

Gotta talk to people live,

And tell 'em that they're cute,

Without the need for them to say,

"You can speak now – UNMUTE!"

Got the Zoomy Blues

Like I never had before,

I'd rather watch the news

And show that Zoom the door,

'Cos I need some human company,

No bloomin' Zoomin' chums for me,

I want 'em close, for sure!

THE LAST WICKET?

Midsummer Eve has passed,

The summer winds blow warm,

Yet this Season and its precursor Spring

Are robbed of Summer's Form.

Even in War the Pavilions were not all shuttered.

The Game was not extinct

If teams could meet.

This year of 2020, a misnomer.

Bereft of sport,

Is wicketless, cricketless,

Lost to all.

Run out before it was begun.

LETTERS FROM A FIRST-YEAR UNIVERSITY STUDENT

Dear Mum and Dad: Greetings from me

In my first great week at university!

I am alive and well, as you can see –

In fact everything's going swimmingly.

It's a beautiful campus with a lake, as you know,

With careful signs showing which way to go

To maintain the proper safety space.

And the guys in my bubble are really ace!

There's no chance of anyone going berserk.

I am dying already to get down to work.

There'll be lectures and seminars, mostly online.

Everything promises to turn out fine!

Greetings from me at uni., Dave.

The Freshers' Week's been a brilliant rave!

Despite the stuff we were told at first,

The official bubbles are easily burst!

I've already met lots of lively guys,

Done an incredible pub crawl (surprise, surprise).

Security blokes try to spoil the fun:

We just bide our time, or hide, or run!

Apparently, I swam in the lake in the dark -

You know me, Dave, up for a (if not with the!) lark!

I somehow got back to my room at half-past four

Without actually having broken the law!

If you see my parents, don't breathe a word!

Me getting drunk? Quite absurd!

I can just imagine their incredulous frown

If they thought I was here still acting the clown.

S S LAMENTATION

Let us raise a prayer for ancient Albion
Now sinking in a plastic sea.

Her past was good and bad in equal measure,
Similar now to you and me.

Though the sea is storm high
And the sky a charcoal hue

Yet now is the time to chart a new course
For the many and not just the few.

So, hold tight me hearties
As we embark from the hard

Because it's better by far than being constantly
Hoisted on our sorry historic petard.

BARDIC THOUGHTS

W-hile a socially-distanced theatre strikes me as heinous

I would like to see a good performance of Coronialanus.

L-ater, Two Gentlemen with Corona – but if R is above 2

L-ike it (As You Do or Don't) we'd see four, eight, sixteen,
and then thirty-two

I-ndividual gents, which would cause delays at the loo

A-ssuming it's open. Coroneo and Juliet could win awards

(M-ake sure the Capulets and Montagues have two-
metre-long swords.

S-horter swords might be issued as new rules are revealed.)

H-amlet, methinks, travelled further afield:

"A-las poor Yuhan! I studied there once, and, to be blunt

K-new at the time the virology lecturer was a c-omplete dunce."

E-ven Oberon and Titania have problems in Athenian
Woods, it's clear:

"S-hut are the toilets and car-parks, there's nothing for
YOU here!"

P-olice bawl, as they fine them (as a last resort), and escort
them out of the county.

E-ven if Puck puts a girdle round the earth in forty
minutes, it's scary-

A-fter he's back, he'll have two weeks of
quarantine, the silly Fairy.

R-emember and be grateful, you blocks, you stones, you worse than senseless things.

E-njoy your time off! If this was fifty years after Shakespeare's death, you'd REALLY

have something to moan about (with a nice big fire the following year).

(And while we're on the subject, why the hell

Can't someone sack that irritating Shrew ..... as well?)

WRITERS AND EDITORS

Once they sat in garrets

With HBs or an Olympus,

To plumb the depth with pencils,

Or rise to heights, typewritten.

The manuscript's the thing.

They'd meet in crowded taverns,

And console each other beerily,

Swop tales of cruel editors,

Discuss fine points of grammar,

The manuscript's the thing.

They never did imagine

That we would save our efforts

In cyberspatial cumulus

To send to our cruel editors

Who famously go bankrupt

In view of such as twitter,

Kindle, Amazon, and blogging,

Now that all can write their pieces,

With no manuscript to fling

Or lose in London taxis.

Though one sole consolation

Is that in the bars and taverns

We can also complain beerily,

And curse the modern editors,

As rejection's still their thing.

ODE DE TOILETTE

I have a shower every day,

Hand-wash constantly, may I say,

With a clean mask daily on my face

I never invade another's space.

Wishing in lockdown to diversify

While in the shower I versify,

Then freshly cologned I finish my ode

Content with another "one for the road".

OVID FOR COVID

In this dreary time of Covid

Why not read the works of Ovid?

The ancient worthy will inspire us

To rise above the wretched virus.

His legendary Ars Amoris

Should regale and rarely bore us;

And we have time to celebrate

A work designed to tittilate.

The virus we can out-fox yet

Without recourse to a box-set

And all of us can enjoy a look

Without staying two metres from the book!

In these days of misery

There's solace here, we can agree:

For who of us feels they're above

The all-enduring art of love

RESPONSE

As a Latinist fastidious

I tend to say Ovidius,

though for us to say Covidius

would be wrong and simply hideous.

Ov's exile on the Black Sea coast

made "ars amoris" at the most

a virtual skill, an idle boast,

the phantom dream of a locked-down ghost.

His "Tristia" groanings and Pontic mail,

his enchanting myths, - tell many a tale

of forms, loves, passions metamorphed

(Most other poets? Simply dwarfed!).

Ov's wondrous works were once the rave,

like pearls of wit from Al or Dave

or centuries scored by cricket men

like Barry Knight or vers(a)tile Ken.

Barry Knight: a formidable all-rounder. Between 1955 & 1969 he scored over 13,000 runs & took over 1,000 wickets. He played 29 Tests & completed the "double" of 1,000 runs & 100 wickets in a season four times for Essex. He was my neighbour, friend and contemporary at the former East Ham Grammar School for Boys in East London - in a different century! (Ron Impey)

A TAD CONFUSED OR BEMUSED

In this strange year of 2020
I find confusions abound in plenty.
I thought I was normal before this year
But some "new normality" now I fear.

When people speak of things as "fake news"
Are they saying all this to simply confuse?
Should the government state what's safe to believe
-Or is that being a trifle naïve?

May I lower my face-mask to gulp down some air
If I'm gasping and generally in despair?
Is my largish family put in a real fix
Now there's decreed the tough rule of six?

They've changed the rules, perhaps, once more,
Leaving me anxious and always unsure.
Though not yet actually out of my mind,
I dread that somehow I might get fined.

Must I drive up to Scotland from here in the West
To find the nearest available test?
It's a lengthy trek to join in the chase
-And will they be able to check or trace?

Gadgets are often a big mystery:
Things just don't seem to work for me.
I'd never be able to spot a "drone"
And even have probs with my mobile phone.

When I see a bright star shining at night,
It might, I am told, be a "satellite".
And, to add to my getting into a flap,
They tell me I must somehow "download a nap"!

In lockdown some folk have got slimmer, some fatter,
But I wonder – in the end does it really matter?
I have no urge left to go off and roam
If it's safer to stay marooned here at home.

Next year must be better, surely, – not worse.
Perhaps I had better soon start to rehearse?

VERA FOREVER

It's a lovely day tomorrow,

Just you wait and see.

There'll be tourists over

From Calais to Dover,

And freedom too for you and me

To travel to meet our folks,

Hug them and tell our jokes.

No more will we be apart

But always together, sweetheart.

When Exeter's Ed gets the last all-clear

The "Tally Ho!" will serve pints of beer

With glorious home-cooked meals

As the old village church bell peals.

We'll go on a bus or train,

The beaches will swarm again (o dear!).

Joy will succeed parting's pain,

We really will meet again

Tomorrow. Just you wait and see!

WELL DONE!

"Say not: the struggle nought availeth".
Not everyone may win the prize
But this we know that we each one may
Achieve the best that in us lies.

Mary Berry has now become a dame;
Baking cakes has brought her fame.
I detect that we are glad to know
That now we can say SIR Hercule Poirot!

Many with names not known to me
Are honoured for their chivalry
Helping others in their need.
Alas, silly poets earn no meed.

I suppose things may look different post-lockdown:
Certain familiar stores we've known closed down?
Hard it is even now to see
Shops like grocers, leathersellers, haberdashery....

Exonerated from every blame
Everyone deserves acclaim
For coping with life that is not the same!

LIGHT AT THE END

When will life be as before?

No fear to walk outside our door.

Will we remember who we were

Before our lives became a blur?

When will we embrace loved ones again?

Once the virus is gone, and only then?

When go out and meet our mates?

When vaccines are working and covid abates?

Will Christmas be normal, or different and strange?

Spending time with family, or speaking from range?

When will we witness the great unmasking?

Breathing the air, standing and basking.

When can we walk without socially spacing

And fretting about the challenge we're facing?

When can we offer a handshake or hug

Without being worried about spreading the bug?

When can we relax in a restaurant or pub

And stop stressing and fretting and rushing our grub?

When can we gather in crowds to watch sport,

Cheering and screaming and giving support –

The range of emotions, the highs and the lows,

But loving the journey, however it goes.

When can we relish live music or arts,

Sharing a passion with joy in our hearts.

When will the count stop of people we've lost,

A world bearing the brunt of emotional cost?

And yet out of the darkness there is still a glimmer

For we have also new life that's starting to shimmer.

The virus won't beat us, we've made that so clear.

There's hope in our future, it's ever so near.

Printed in Great Britain
by Amazon